Inheritance

The

Quintessential, Firebrand, Prophetic and Streetwise

Poetry from the son of a Preacher Man

Inheritance

The

Quintessential, Firebrand, Prophetic and Streetwise

Poetry from the son of a Preacher Man

by
Brother James

Senior Publisher
Steven Lawrence Hill Sr.

Awarded Publishing House
ASA Publishing Company
Established Since 2005

A Publisher Trademark Cover page

ASA Publishing Company
Awarded Best Publisher for Quality Books 2008, 2009
105 E. Front St., Suite 201A, Monroe, Michigan 48161
United States of America
www.asapublishingcompany.com

All Rights Reserved. No part of this publication may be reproduced, stored in a retrieval system or transmitted in any form or by any means electronic, mechanical, photocopying, recording, taping, web distribution, information storage, or otherwise, without the prior written permission of the publisher. Author/writer rights to "Freedom of Speech" protected by and with the "1st Amendment" of the Constitution of the United States of America. This poetry is a work of religious educational and historical learning purposes. With this title page, the reader is notified that this text is an educational tool in poetic form, and the publisher does not assume, and expressly disclaims any obligation to obtain and/or include any other information other than that provided by the author. Any belief system, promotional motivations, including but not limited to the use of non-fiction characters and/or characteristics of this book, are within the boundaries of the author's own creativity and/or testimony in order to reflect the nature and concept of the book.

Any and all vending sales and distribution not permitted without full book cover and this title page.

Copyrights©2012 Henry James (Brother James), All Rights Reserved
Book: Inheritance *"The Quintessential, Firebrand, Prophetic and Streetwise Poetry from the son of a Preacher Man"*

Date Published: 04.18.12
Edition: 1 *Trade Paperback*
Book ASAPCID: 2380595
ISBN: 978-1-886528-28-4
Library of Congress Cataloging-in-Publication Data

This book was published in the United States of America.
State of Michigan

A Publisher Trademark Title page

Table of Contents

Inheritance
"The Quintessential, Firebrand, Prophetic and Streetwise Poetry from the son of a Preacher Man"

Poem	Date Written	Page
Dedication		i
Foreword		iii
To be a Poet	08/08/77	1
Addicted	10/03/76	1
Vibrations	10/03/76	1
A Tribute to African Women	10/15/76	2
African Queen	09/27/77	4
Midnight Blues	08/08/76	5
Now that you've turned your back on me	10/03/76	6
Dialogue	10/06/76 and 03/08/97	7
Politics	10/06/76	8
Where Are All the Brothers	08/08/76 and 08/08/90	9
Brenda	07/15/81	10
Cadence: A Military Marching Song	03/08/82	11
Guided Missiles, Misguided Men	04/30/82	12
Africa is Our Land	12/29/77	13
We've got to get Ourselves Together	12/29/79	15
Ebony Woman I Love You	08/08/76	17
Reality	08/08/76	18
Ebony King	12/10/77	19
We Met in a Dream	10/04/78	20
Pain	10/03/76	21
Sisters and Brothers	05/15/78	22
No More Pride	12/20/77	23

So Fine	08/08/78	24
Coloured Students	08/08/76	24
A Poem For A Lady I'd Like To Know	10/08/78	25
No Parts of Love	12/29/78	26
Inheritance	02/08/97	28
Love ain't nothing but another Word for Dementia	08/08/95	29
How is it that...????	08/08/96	30
What would Dr. King think?	11/20/90	31
Co$t of Living	08/08/77	33
I Want to Wait!	06/08/96	34
Something about you...	11/29/96	35
To Arthia on the Passing of Your Mother	02/12/97	36
OPM: Other People's Money	06/08/96	37
My Lady	02/20/97	38
To Woody on the Passing of Your Mother	12/08/96	38
Gettin' Off	12/05/96	39
He Said/She Said	03/08/97	40
Focus on the Positives	12/29/94	41
Back in the Day	03/18/97	42
Black Robed Blues	06/08/78	43
I want to mend your Broken Heart	05/15/01	44
Some Sista's wouldn't know a good brother if they tripped over Him!	08/08/99	46
Relationships: The Good, The Bad, and The Ugly	06/10/01	48
He Just Keeps on Blessing Me!	08/08/02	50
Let Me Live My Life	08/08/03	52
When I Think of YOU	08/08/04	53
True Love Ain't Conditional	08/08/07	53
Your Cousins	08/08/07	55
Haters	08/04/07	58
Medgar Evers Died for Your Sins	08/08/00	60
She likes the Brotha's	10/28/06	62
My X's: A Poem Dedicated to the Composite of Some of the Women I Have Dated	12/13/06	64
Should I?	12/29/06	66

Dedication

In traditional African society it was customary to ALWAYS begin any ceremony or dedication with a tribute to ones ancestors. Therefore as an African in the diaspora I lovingly dedicate this book to the memory of the following African Queens:

Momma Molly, my maternal great-grandmother, Mother Porter, my maternal grandmother, Mother James, my paternal grandmother

Mrs. Webbie, my first grade teacher whose love and concern for me at such an early age whetted what has developed into an insatiable appetite for knowledge and;

The late Mrs. Campbell, a member of the Hill Street Baptist Church in my hometown, Louisville, Kentucky, whose ever present smile and constant encouragement provided me with an incentive for public speaking.

I dedicate this book to the memory of the following African Kings:

Poppa, my maternal great-grandfather, Daddy Sylvester my maternal grandfather, Daddy Willie, my paternal grandfather.

Elbert Williams, my mentor in Washington, DC who showed me how to survive in the jungle, the gladiatorial arena that is the Federal Government.

I also especially dedicate this book to:

My Mother, Mrs. Juanita M. James. Momma you are truly one in a Trillion. God truly blessed me by placing me in your loving care. Even though you have made your transition to Heaven you are still here with me. I love you.

Dorcas and Carolyn my two beautiful sisters
Ramonda, Robyn, Shannon, Chenille, and Gwen my five beautiful nieces
Leanna, Annie Jean, Alberta (Deceased), Hilda (Deceased), Mary Lena (Deceased), Norma, Wilhelmina, Sylvia (Deceased), and Billie my aunts.

All my female first and second cousins - TOO numerous to mention by name.

My three adopted sisters; Valerie Cavanaugh, Anna McGuire who proved that somebody will love you when you are down and out. Thanks Anna I will never ever forget you. Maisah Robinson. Maisah your principles, integrity and odd sense of humor kept me going while I was a Gladiator in the academic arena known as the Ohio State University.

TO WOMEN OF AFRICAN DESCENT EVERYWHERE!

Foreword

This book has been a long time in the making. I was prohibited for many years from publishing my works due to an "Honoria Ban" unfairly imposed on all Federal Government employees. I never stopped writing; always believing that one-day the Honoria Ban would be lifted. Well it has and I am ever so proud to present to you what some might term trite poetry, and that is okay. I am reminded of a quote attributed to Malcolm X, who said, "never use fifty cent words with people who have a ten cent education." My point simply put is that I write to reach the broadest possible audience. If others want to create esoteric works that is their right, but as for me I write to be read and understood by everyone. So if you find my works elementary that to is okay, but someone out there will enjoy the themes and messages inherent in my works. I speak to the hearts and minds of the average person who is faced day in and day out with the adversities of life in an ever changing society. I also write for my people for I am part of a historical continuum known as the Griot Tradition. A Griot in traditional West African society was a story teller, an Oral Historian. The walking talking repository of his particular ethnic groups history and culture. What you will find in this book is a historical and evolutionary look at life, Black life in the Western context. Therefore herein lies a collection of poems which I tend to believe are universal to the African American experience. These poems having been written by an African in the diaspora express the hopes, fears, joys, loves, sadness, bitterness and aspirations of a people who by an unfortunate act in history, namely the African

Slave Trade are forced to unconsciously and sometimes consciously aspire to the values systems and culture imposed upon them by a socioeconomic system that views them as being expendable objects. It is this same cultural system that relegates the African American to being a history-less and culturally deprived people. Some may find my poetry offensive. That is not my intent. As a Griot I am like the CNN of my community. It is my responsibility to report what I see in the hope that my people will divorce themselves from self defacing and self destructive behaviors. By no means do I purport to be the final arbitrator of all the is right and wrong for the African in the diaspora, for I am not without faults and errors in judgment, By no means do I say that everything that is happening to the African American is negative, for there are positives and negatives in everything. What I do say however is this, as a people we must stress the importance of knowing our history, for as it is written, "he who does not know his history is doomed to repeat it." Herein lies a message to my people; we must love one another, we must protect one another, and we must get involved in any positive organization to combat any and all trends, policies, and acts whether they be overt or covert that adversely affects us. Herein lies some of my innermost thoughts. And herein lies MY TRUTH.

Brother James (*Henry James*)

Author's Note: The poems within this piece of literature should be viewed in terms of the context of the times in which they were written. HJ

Inheritance

The

Quintessential, Firebrand, Prophetic and Streetwise

Poetry from the son of a Preacher Man

by
Brother James

To Be A Poet

Straining my brain
a poem to create
about to go insane
cause my ideas won't relate
but to be a poet is my desire
so a message I must impart
my words should set my people's minds on fire
and put love within their hearts

ADDICTED

I'm addicted to a Black woman full of love,
My addiction for her was designed from above,
Of my love for her I'm very sure,
And I'd kill anyone who found a cure,
Just to be with this beautiful sister I'd perform any deed,
Because she's all that I want and all that I need.

VIBRATIONS

Strong vibrations from a body so sleek,
Intense vibrations that leave me weak,
Vibrations from a love so fine,
Vibrations from a sister, who's blowing my mind,
Intellectual vibrations that enlighten me,
Spiritual vibrations that set me free,
Vibrations that constantly send me to a higher plane,
Baby, if I were to lose these vibrations
I'd go insane

A TRIBUTE TO AFRICAN WOMEN

Daughters of Africa you are both creator and Queen
But rarely in the pages of history are your accomplishments seen
The oppressor, the exploiter, has made it his lifelong duty
To hide from the world your legacy of bravery, devotion and outstanding beauty
The image the oppressor projects of you, is one intended to generate shame
But history, properly recorded, would indicate you warrant international fame
Candace of Ethiopia, Nefertiti of Egypt, and Nzinga of Angola only to name a few
Are highly representative of the fine qualities which are reflected in you
Dispersed to the western hemisphere to slave within America's shores
You fought alongside your man in what they call slave revolts,
but what were in reality national liberation wars
Raped, beaten, degraded, forced to work from "can't see in the morning" to "can't see at night"
No matter how bad you were treated you never gave up the fight
Harriet Tubman, Sojourner Truth, Ida B. Wells and Fannie Lou Hamer are just part of your tradition
Because you have always been in the forefront of your peoples struggles against adverse conditions
On the African continent your struggles were somewhat unique
For you fought, bled, and died for freedom in Angola, Guineau Bisseau and Mozambique

Throughout the Caribbean you've raised your voice
against poverty and an inadequate diet
You were on the frontline of what the press called the
Caribbean's Black Power riots
Therefore, I have no reservation, the following to declare
When considered with the world's other women you are
definitely degrees beyond compare

AFRICAN QUEEN

BEAUTIFUL AFRICAN WOMAN OF THE NILE
ENCHANTING AND CAPTIVATING ME WITH YOUR SMILE
YOUR MIND IS SO TOGETHER AND YOUR BODY'S SO FINE
JUST SEEING YOU WALKING BY NEARLY BLOWS MY MIND
TO BE WITH YOU AND ONLY YOU FOREVER IS MY DESIRE
AND OF THIS LOVE I EXPRESS FOR YOU I HOPE YOU'LL NEVER TIRE
THERE IS NO DOUBT - ABSOLUTELY - POSITIVELY IN MY MIND
THAT LADIES WITH ALL YOUR QUALITIES ARE INDEED A RARE FIND
THEREFORE I KNOW WHEN I'VE GOT A GOOD THING
SO AS MY AFRICAN QUEEN TO YOU MY LOVE AND DEVOTION I'LL CONSTANTLY BRING
I'VE SEEN ALL THE OTHER WOMEN UNDER THE SUN
AND AMONG THEM YOU ARE MOST DEFINITELY NUMBER ONE
WHEN IT COMES TO WOMEN SOME MEN ARE FILLED WITH GREED
BUT AIN'T NO HAPPENINGS HERE BECAUSE YOU'RE ALL THAT I NEED
AND LOVING YOU IS MY LIFELONG RESOLUTION

BECAUSE TO ME FOR YOU THERE IS NO
SUBSTITUTION
SO AS WE DEAL WITH LIFE'S PROBLEMS
HAND IN HAND
NEVER FORGET FOR AS LONG AS WE
BOTH SHALL LIVE THAT I AM YOU MAN

Midnight Blues

Been down, oh so low
where looking up was down
how long I've had the blues I do not know
and I'm tired of wearing a frown
but my baby man, she don't care
cause she's the one that's giving me the blues
I've always shown her a love beyond compare
but my kindness she won't hesitate to abuse
well you go your way Lady, and I'll go mine
cause the time has come for us to part
and all wounds are said to heal with time
but I'll be damned if you'll break my heart

NOW THAT YOU'VE TURNED YOUR BACK ON ME

Your call last night
really blew my mind
your intention was to start a fight
the reasons for which I couldn't find
you accused me of lying
and said you had been deceived
but all along I've been trying
to show you the misery that I've received
by being faithful and always giving you my undivided attention
and in your corner when you were down
but my reward was however, jealously and suspicion
and I'm at the point of even leaving town
because above all I needed you to understand
that I was yours and only your devoted man

DIALOGUE

Hey man
You know
I just saw your lady
You know
With this other <u>BAAADD</u> lady
You know
So I thought I'd conversate with her
You know
And I got the digits
You know
But she's got a man already
You know
Check this
You know
I just might make that lady mine
You know
If only I could just tease her, please her, and squeeze her
You know
You know I'm the Man
You know
And I can pull her my way
You Know
I hope my thing with this sister I don't blow
By always saying
You know
You know
You know

POLITICS

Politics in America are just a game,
because after voting my material conditions are the same,
Given the right to vote at eighteen,
only prior to election day can the politicians be seen,
In my neighborhood,
telling me of their good,
Ideas, intentions and master plan,
that will put more dollars in my hand,
This I can truly see
politicians are trying to make a fool of me

Where Are All the Brothers?

From the war of independence to World War two
many strong Black men have died for you
even in Korea and Vietnam
a lot of brothers died for Uncle Sam

Where Are All the Brothers?
In our neighborhoods coke and heroin are easily found
to a lifetime of addiction many young brothers are bound
Brothers O-D-ing from too much DOPE
beautiful sisters slowly losing hope
Where Are All the Brothers?

Living in ghettoes with seldom more than a dime
young brothers from the ages of 8-12 starting a life of crime
brothers robbing and stealing just to pay their rent
and in all your prisons brothers account for 75 percent
Where Are All the Brothers?

Beautiful sisters in all shapes, sizes and colors from
ebony to tan
all in an endless search to find a kind, strong, Black man
beautiful sisters at a party dressed as fine as can be
but the ratio of Brothers to Sisters is one to three

Where Are All the Brothers?
Where Are All the Brothers?
Where Are All the Brothers?

BRENDA

Brenda's ancestors worked in massa's house down on the plantation
had no problems entering VASSAR and HARVARD to get her education
now she makes big bucks working for a major corporation
BUT BRENDA DOESN'T HAVE A MAN!

BRENDA
and her running partners are the local jet set
her "BREEDING" and "INTELLECT" truly are her best assets
a charming, amusing personality that makes her impossible to forget
BUT BRENDA DOESN'T HAVE A MAN!

BRENDA says
"my man MUST be tall, well educated, and handsome,
a professional with a very-very high in-income,
who can provide the lifestyle to which I am accustomed"
BUT BRENDA DOESN'T HAVE A MAN!

BRENDA'S problem,
is that she REFUSES to date
a brother who isn't college educated and a fashion-plate
only someone on HER LEVEL can qualify as her helpmate
I hope she'll re-access her criteria before it's too LATE
BECAUSE BRENDA DOESN'T HAVE A MAN!

CADENCE:
A MILITARY MARCHING SONG

Johnny's going off to war
HEY! HEY!
possibly in some Afghanistan province called Kandahar
HEY! HEY!
Johnny's going off to war
just because he's Black and poor
BAY-OH-BAY-BEE mine
Go to you left - your right -your left
Go to you left - your right - your left
Johnny's folks are awful sad
HEY! HEY!
Cause Johnny came home in a BODY BAG!
HEY! HEY!
got a cable saying: "Johnny died like a man,
in addition for your loss here's a check for 10 Grand"
BAY-OH-BAY-BEE mine
Go to you left - your right -your left
Go to you left - your right - your left
Well this here poem's coming to an end
HEY! HEY!
The point I'm trying to make is it's really a sin
HEY! HEY!
That America send its poorest youth to die in foreign Wars
But never really explains what they're dying for!
BAY-OH-BAY-BEE mine
Go to you left - your right -your left
Go to you left - your right - your left
WHAT HAVE ALL THE BROTHERS DIED FOR-
FIGHTING FOR AMERICA-ANYWAY?

GUIDED MISSILES - MISGUIDED MEN

One bomb, two bombs, three bombs, four
People counting bombs instead of sheep
Worried about another country's having more
Hydrogen, neutron, kilo or megaton
Once the first one's dropped
Will it really matter who WON?
Western Europe praying that the U.S. and
Russia will not make a mistake
Being caught in the middle, their entire future's at stake
From the attack - counter attack, nuclear debris over the
ENTIRE world will spread
Catastrophic end results - not enough survivors to even
bury the dead
To many a nuclear war is imminent and it's really a sin
That so much time and energy is spent on guided
missiles by misguided men

AFRICA IS OUR LAND!

It must be common knowledge and by now most Black folks must know
that the Leakeys found the oldest human remains in East Attica dating back 3.5 million years ago
and the most learned historians have begun to note
that Africans from "Guinea" were here to greet Columbus when he got off his boat
the history of African people has been distorted and hid
and it is no mere coincidence that the ruins of the Aztecs, Incas and Mayans closely resemble those of an Egyptian pyramid
little mention if any in history is made, of how Africans called the MOORS
improved the Dutch, English, Spanish and Portuguese societies, commerce, and trade to the western hemisphere shores
Liz Taylor played Cleopatra! won't the motion picture industry run us no slack?
Because in reality Cleopatra, Nefertiti, and most of the Pharaohs were Black!
And as early as 1619 in this country we arrived
and from the fruits of Black folks labor America grew, prospered, and thrived
Slave, Nigger, Colored, negro all were my name
Hey, don't you have any pity or shame??
because in "64 in Birmingham, 4 Blacks girls in a church you blew away
only ONE white man has been tried and convicted for that crime to this very day
Emmit Till, James Chaney, Malcolm, Medgar, Martin and numerous other Black people you have killed

but when we burnt L.A., Detroit, and D.C. to the ground,
the scars of racism you wanted healed
in '68 the votes Nixon got over McGovern were extremely high
and while Nixon was in office many brothers were sent to Vietnam to be maimed and to die
but after seven years in office Tricky Dick was replaced by Mr. Peanut, Jimmy Carter
and now America's declining position is evident, because with her former enemies she must barter
and all barter is in this world is trade
now unemployment in this country which is very high
because fewer U.S. exploited dollars are being made
because the Arabs control the oil and the racist regime in South Africa was thrown out
and the population of this country will continue to have to do without
because all of Africa's oil, diamonds, copper, uranium, and gold
will be controlled by positive and progressive Africans when the final story has been told
For Africa is our land and we won't rest or give you any mercy or slack
Until Black folk the world over are free of exploitation and have taken Attica BACK!!

WE HAVE GOT TO GET OURSELVES TOGETHER

ghetto streets becoming gang combat zones on Saturday night
as young brothers bleed from being cut, shot, and stabbed in a big gang fight
Black mothers worrying themselves sick
because their young daughters are turning tricks
WE HAVE GOT TO GET OURSELVES TOGETHER

Black folk with unlimited potential giving up hope
trying to hide their fears and frustrations by using dope
Black parents trying their best to keep their kids safe from harm
while a 12 year old junkie lies dead with a needle in his arm
WE HAVE GOT TO GET OURSELVES TOGETHER

Pimps, whores, pushers all living on easy street
their own sisters and brothers they don't hesitate to beat
young sisters and brothers beating up their teachers in school
destined to grow up to become nothing but uneducated fools
WE HAVE GOT TO GET OURSELVES TOGETHER

For chump change NEGROES are down at the pig pen squealing
so that our true and courageous leaders the cops will soon be killing
NEGROES in high level positions constantly kissing white folks ass

not giving any thought to why the bulk of their people are in the lower class
WE HAVE GOT TO GET OURSELVES TOGETHER

Finely dressed NEGRO preachers, preaching that we will get our reward in heaven
while drugs, poverty, and inner city isolation keep most of us from reaching the age of 57
Kool-Aid, candy bars, neck bones and chittlin's make up our diet
if Black folks really knew what we ate we'd have a DIET RIOT
WE HAVE GOT TO GET OURSELVES TOGETHER

My problems are your problems and your problems are mine
we've got to stop killing one another and end Black on Black crime
We must unite the whole world over and come together as one
In order that we might assume our proper dignity and place under the sun

WE HAVE GOT TO GET OURSELVES TOGETHER
WE HAVE GOT TO GET OURSELVES TOGETHER
WE HAVE GOT TO GET OURSELVES TOGETHER!!!

EBONY WOMAN I LOVE YOU

Loving Black women so dear and kind
You are my pillar of strength and you ease my mind
Always there in my hour of need
Producing beautiful Ebony children from my seed

EBONY WOMAN I LOVE YOU

The love you are so full of knocks me off my feet
And everything you do, to, with, and for me makes me feel so complete
The love you give to me I can't help but reflect
And as long as I live you'll always have my ultimate respect

EBONY WOMAN I NEED YOU

It is because of someone like you that I am alive
And to be a major part of your life I'll always strive
Ebony woman you mean so much to me
And to the lock of my heart, you possess the only key.

Reality

Who do you think you are fooling when you smile to hide a frown,
Pretending that your spirits are up when you know they are really down,
Who do you think you are fooling when you say that you don't care,
While in reality you hope to rid yourself of this anguish that you bear,
Who do you think you are fooling when you say you'll find someone new,
When in reality it was your actions that have left you sad and blue,
Who do you think you are fooling when you hide your fears in dope,
Please wake up and realize that coping with reality is your only hope,
For if in <u>DRUGS</u> you intend to find a cure,
You are as good as dead and that's for sure,
Please heed my words and believe me when I say,
That coping with reality, is the **ONLY WAY**

Ebony King

From the motherland of all civilizations
you were the builders of the world's foremost nations
on the AFRIKAN continent you were historian, builder, and king
so when enslaved to the "new world" all you culture and skills you did bring
enduring slavery's cruel sting you kept your pride
and often times you died trying to protect the Ebony Queen at your side
to you no credit is given for building this land
and even though denied your heritage you stood tall like a man
father, protector, and leader you've always been
because the Pharaohs
Nat Turner
Fredrick Douglass
Dubois
Randolph
Nkrumah
Garvey
King and
Malcolm
were all truly wise and great Black MEN!!

WE MET IN A DREAM

We met in a dream
and you were the EPITOME
of loveliness and beauty
we met in a dream
and you were
the conglomeration
of INTELLIGENCE
STRENGTH and
CHARACTER
We met in a dream
and you were the reflection in action of
NEFERTITI
HARRIET TUBMAN
FANNIE LOU HAMER
and so many other
BEAUTIFUL and COURAGEOUS daughters of mother
AFRICA
we met in a dream
and you were BLACK WOMAN
we met in a dream
and you were
my REALITY
and my DESTINY
for I came from you
and whatever I accomplish
in this life
IOU
we met in a dream
and dreaming of you
has given me
my ultimate

Reason for living
and to you I shall
ALWAYS
be OBLIGATED
my dreams
MUST
become
not MY
but OUR
REALITY
for I LOVE YOU
BEAUTIFUL BLACK WOMAN

PAIN

The loss of a love that was so true,
the realization of all my faults in losing you,
a player of all the ladies I tried to be,
but a fool I was and now I see,
True to you I should have stayed,
instead of seeking more women to be laid,
you were always around in my hour of need,
but now I've lost you because of my ego and greed,
I know it's too late to ask for one more chance,
that I a fool and you could rebuild a true romance.

SISTERS AND BROTHERS

Sister-Sister with your hair that's fried
Sister-Sister with your hair that's dyed
Sister-Sister where's your pride?
Because beauty is something that should come from within
And the imitation of others is the greatest sin
The image of other women shouldn't be your goal
Can't you see that you're slowly losing your soul?
Well one day soon I truly hope that you'll find
That the most beautiful black women are of the natural kind. . .
Brother-Brother with your rap so weak
Why is it the white man's woman that you seek?
And why is it becoming so apparent of late
that with beautiful black women you can't relate
Brother-Brother with your processed head
Your only status is your 3-piece threads
Brother-Brother why not use your charm
To put a fine beautiful black woman on your arm
Because to a black woman you have an obligation to love and protect
Because above all we need UNITY-POWER-and SELF-RESPECT!

No More Pride

No More Pride
Our African heritage we try to hide
No More Pride
All notions of Black Unity we've put aside
No More Pride
Forgetting about Marcus, Malcolm, Medgar, and Martin and why they died
No More Pride
No longer do we want our brothers and sisters by our side
No More Pride
Our values and greedy white folks values beginning to coincide
No More Pride
Our only goal in life is to drive a brand new ride
No More Pride
Beginning to believe the lie's of the man we know has always lied
No More Pride
On some means of UNITY we must all soon decide
No More Pride
Because we must come together the world over in our political stride
Or we will be doomed forever to be a people with
No More Pride

So Fine

a permanent relationship with you I want to bind
So Fine
one mind in two bodies and two bodies physically entwined
So Fine
that no other Lady could replace you with a jive ass line
So Fine
you're so pretty and sweet and Oh, so kind
So Fine
ain't nothing or nobody gonna get you off my mind
So Fine
that as we grow old together our love will mellow like an expensive wine
So Fine

COLOURED STUDENTS

Your Black teachers have to beg you to do their work,
Your answer is I'm Black and should be allowed to shirk,
For your business or English teacher you use your mind,
But for anything Black the time you can't seem to find,
If in business or finance you get an E
To your white instructor you cop a plea
But when given an E in things that are Black,
Your instructor you want to see placed on the rack,
It seems my brother that you fail to see,
That knowledge of yourself should be your first priority.

A POEM FOR A LADY THAT I'D LIKE TO KNOW

to become acquainted with you I am compelled to try
since the day your warm and sincere smile first caught my eye
you are so physically beautiful that it is almost a sin
and your poise, your grace, indicates that you are equally beautiful within
I am completely awe struck by you and I feel it is a shame that I have not been <u>BOLD</u> enough to ask your name
please do not misunderstand my intentions as you read this rhyme
for we could become the best of friends in a very short time
the inference that I hope that you will draw as this poem comes to an end
is that I; Brother James wish to become your friend

NO PARTS OF LOVE

If love is constantly being abused
  THEN I WANT NO PARTS OF LOVE
If love is being loving and generous but not having my love
  and generosity returned
  THEN I WANT NO PARTS OF LOVE
  If love means being lied to time and time again
  THEN I WANT NO PARTS OF LOVE
  If love is a true commitment between us but I am
  Constantly without you
  THEN I WANT NO PARTS OF LOVE
  If love is my having to always prove my love for you
  THEN I WANT NO PARTS OF LOVE
  If love is my having to be hurt again and again
  by someone that I love - and I do mean Y-O-U
THEN I WANT NO PARTS OF LOVE
 But if love is living together with you forever and a day in peace and happiness
 with our mutual love growing stronger as each and every day passes
 And if love is my loving you and you
 loving me and my needing you
 because I love you
 And if love is our love being
 So together that poems
 Songs, novels and
 plays could and
 Should be
 written
 about it.

*And if love is our relationship being
the epitome of devotion, loyalty
and sincerity*
THEN I WANT ALL THE LOVE I CAN GET

Inheritance

from my Mother's Mother I inherited my dimpled smile and determination
from my Father's Mother I inherited my gift for writing, my sense of family dedication
from my Mother's Father I inherited my thirst to travel to places I've never been
from my Father's Father I inherited my charm, manners, how to be a true gentleman
from my Mother I inherited my intellect, intuition, compassion for people I may never meet
from my Father I inherited my stamina, my religion, and from a principled position never retreat
from my Parents and Grandparents I have learned many lessons on how to live
but most important of all the lessons they taught me were how to love and forgive
to love those who would forsake me while steadfastly claiming to be my friend
to forgive those who smile in my face but the moment I turn my back try to do me in
to love those who tell everyone they encounter they have the "411" on me
to forgive them of their pettiness, ignorance, because the real me they will never see
my ancestors taught me many lessons on how to live, and taught me well
that only to a select few do you share your innermost thoughts, my secrets to never tell
some may view me as naive, innocent, weird, or even a fool

but I was taught to distinguish who truly loves me, who only wants me to be their tool
I am at that point in life where I don't care what others think of me,
I really don't give a damn
Because I am Proud to be descended from my folks,
Proud of who and what I am

Love ain't nothing but another word for Dementia

I used to think I *was* in love
with a beautiful angel sent to me from above
but the reality is I *was* in complete and total lust
with a deep, dark chocolate sister, with an incredible bust
I used to think that I had found someone who *was* within my social and intellectual reach
when I met this Carmel colored, statuesque sister, a Georgia Peach
but my reality *was* that she was not wrapped too tight
because she changed her mind about who she loved both day and night
I then met a sister to whom I could truly relate
but this sister *was* already taken, involved, DAMN! - I *was* TOO late
it just seems too hard to embark on a positive relationship
I guess that's why falling in love for most of us is a major trip
I now feel that my definition of what true love is, is a little hazy
I'm now of the opinion, that to want to fall in love TODAY, one must truly be CRAZY!! !

How is it that... ????

how is it that you can care for someone and love them so much
that you could be 100's of miles apart and still feel their touch
how is it that you could hold someone so near to your heart
that you would yearn for them every second you were apart
how is it that you always daydream of this special person you miss
that you would walk, no run a hundred miles to see them just for a hug and a kiss
how is it that God has blessed, ordained you with a love from above
that you'd have a nearly perfect relationship, totally saturated with love
how is it that you trust one another so much when you are apart
that doubts, suspicions, nor jealousy never enter your heart
how is it that I have found the ultimate love, a love so true
that is why I know that Almighty God blessed me by leading me to YOU!

What would Dr. King think?

Whatever happened to the DREAM
of Dr. Martin Luther King
that from "sea to shining sea"
we would ALL be totally immersed in...
this elusive thing called EQUALITY
if Dr. King were alive today
I wonder what he would have to say
about the ill will that is RAPIDLY spreading across this land
particularly the RISE instead of DEMISE of the Klu Klux Klan
Is it possible that Dr. King would think it nothing but a flux
that in <u>1990</u> the U. S. House barely missed seating david duke?
would Dr. King wonder WHO is diligently leading the fight
to ELIMINATE the economic disparity between Black and White?
would he question the leaders of the "Sweet Land of Liberty"
about WHY there are STILL so many Poor, Illiterate,
and Homeless as far as the eye can see?
would Dr. King be concerned that in "The land of the free
and home of the Brave"
this nations drug policy offers no clear cut solutions ...
our future generations to save?
do you think he would question - Why in the "Land of the Pilgrims Pride"
people not only in the ghetto, but on Wall Street, at ALL levels of
government and EVEN in the <u>Ministry</u> use Cocaine their
fears, and weaknesses to hide?

would Dr. King ask WHY hundreds of thousands of America's youth are routinely being sent to foreign shores to possibly be maimed, mentally rearranged and killed in Undeclared Wars?
Would Dr. King be disappointed and think it a downright shame
that the people of Arizona would rather lose millions, possibly billions than to have a PAID holiday to honor his name?
Well this is what I believe Dr. King would think
that America is socio-economically, politically and morally on the brink
of an irreversible and catastrophic decline
UNLESS the people of good will and conscience step forward ...
a positive solution to find!
the people in this country of every race, color, and creed must make a determined stand
to eliminate, eradicate ALL the adverse conditions impacting this land
because "united we stand and divided we fall"
when Dr. King spoke of equality he meant equality NOT for SOME but for ALL!
Therefore we MUST make this country practice what it preaches!
About fair play, honesty and all the other attributes to the rest of the world it teaches
It is IMPERATIVE that one day from every valley and mountain top a national chorus will sing
Let Freedom Reign! ... Let Freedom Reign! ... Let Freedom Reign!

Co$t of Living

The cost of living in this country has gone to the extreme and many people have given up on the "Great American Dream"
it's so hard these days just to make ends meet
and maintaining a decent savings account is becoming quite a feat
it used to be said that higher education would improve one's condition
but many Ph. D's are competing with each other over many a low paying position
and the landlords are raising their rents higher each and every day
so high that many families become nomads because of their inability to pay
even if you've got the cash to pay your rent your condition is still unreal
because the money used to pay the rent was also needed for the gas and electric bill
the rising price of gasoline should really make you want to holler
because the price of one gallon of regular will soon exceed five dollars
the anger among shoppers in the groceries may eventually cause a riot
and it appears that soon we all we be on a bread and water diet
and going to the doctor or dentist definitely ain't no thrill
it isn't the pain so much you fear but being the recipient of their bill
well as the rich get richer and the poor get poorer
this country's rapidly heading toward a new social order

and as quiet as it's kept, and just between you and me these greedy politicians and captains of industry have really messed up the world's economy

I Want to Wait!

Some would say that I'm the world's biggest fool
because I want to wait before I lay with you
Some might say, "man can't you see that she's ready"
but I want to wait until we're deeply in love, a love that's secure and steady
I know as we get closer the time or times will be right
but I want to wait and resist my physical urges for you with all my might
you must not think that I don't desire you, and you must understand
that I want to wait because for you I want to forever be a perfect and Godly man
please don't get me wrong, I certainly want to lay with you for the rest of my life
but I want to wait, until we are truly in love and you've decided to be my wife

Something about you....

I was in a self-imposed Exile
for a very long while
then your eyes met mine
I knew it was time
myself to release
to find true love, an inner peace
with you
it's true
because there's something about you....
something that makes my body quake
my arms and legs tremble, my heartache
my eyes flutter, I'm forced to stutter
previously articulate now I only mutter
because there's something about you....
you are my African Queen
no one comparable exist on the scene
yours is a love others can't duplicate
if someone were to imply you're not for me I'd become
irate
because there's something about you....
you make me drop my defenses built from past memories
of love gone bad that created deceptions, indiscretions,
assorted agonies
you have made me want to fall madly, deeply in love
again
you're always there, from chaos to bliss, you are my very
best friend
because there's something about you....
I thank and praise God daily for having you in my life
If you haven't figured it out by now I want you for my wife
I want to grow old with you, my love for you is for real

a love that's like pouring water into a cup that never, ever overfills
because there's something about you ....

To Arthia on the Passing of Your Mother

Your Mother has met Saint Peter at the Pearly Gate
This was one meeting you'd postpone, but the Lord could no longer wait
To take your Mother into his loving arms to provide her with eternal rest and peace
To take away all her worldly burdens, and from her physical pains he's given her a release
She is looking down on all of you who in this physical existence remain
She wants you to know that she has truly been delivered, and she's not feeling any pain
Let her memory guide you and those she held in this life so dear
Think only of the good times spent together, and remember she's always near
Near to your heart, your mind, your soul
She wants you to continue to make getting closer to the Lord your goal
Because she's in the presence of the Angels basking in the glow of God's undying Love
And she is waiting for the day that you will be reunited in heaven above

OPM: Other People's Money

other people who have no knowledge of your financial condition
will be the first to tell you how to spend the money you work for, like they were on a mission
they'll tell you about the fashion designer clothes they'd wear if they made your kind of cash
all the money they'd spend on their entourage without having to dip into their stash
the sport or luxury cars they'd drive, the BIG house they'd live in
the monthly worldwide jaunts they'd go on, especially weekends in the Caribbean
oh they'll tell you how if they were in your shoes they'd take everyone out to lunch
because certainly someone who makes what you make can't be in a financial crunch
what they do not realize is that no matter how much you earn your spending patterns are relative
you have a cash flow problem just like they do, it's within our means that we all try to live
so tell them that if they didn't go to your job everyday and deal with all the stress and nonsense
they should stop trying to spend others people's money, and mind their own damn business

My Lady

My lady doesn't have to cook for me
or always try to look pretty like Halle Berry or Pam on "Martin," consistently
My lady doesn't have to be sitting, waiting on my every "beck and call"
SHE can do her own thing, I want my lady to be herself: and stand Tall
My lady doesn't have to laugh at my jokes she KNOWS aren't Funny
She' confident, her own woman, she makes HER Own money
My lady doesn't ever have to pretend, she's definitely Heaven sent
You see, my lady is naturally Beautiful, and most importantly she's INDEPENDENT!!!

To Woody on the Passing of Your Mother

Your **Mother** has moved on to a higher plane
where she's content, at rest, and not feeling any pain
she would want you to relish in the memories that you both held so dear
let her heavenly spirit guide you, know that she's always near
God's grace and **Time** will eventually heal both your loss and your pain
and please rest assured knowing that one day - you and your **Mother** will meet again

Gettin' Off

some people get off on the expensive clothes they wear
others get off from the exotic, erotic designs on their fingernails, their hair
then there are those who get off on their Audi's, Porcshe's, their Mercedes Benz
they brag about how much the houses cost in the neighborhoods they live in,
but they never realize that material things always come and go
finding a way to get closer to God is what they truly need to know
because without the Lord in their life
they'll only find loneliness, misery, and endless days full of strife
we all need to heed the Lord's wake up call, to stand tall, endeavor not to sin
I know that God is telling us something, but most of us are not listening.

He Said/She Said

Bzzzzzzzzzz went their alarm clock at 5:30 in the morning
He said, "Boo hit the snooze button, I need 4 more hours of sleep,
as he was stretching and yawning
She said, "BABY" you need to get up and start looking for a J-O-B
cause I can't continue to be the *only one* in this house bringing in any money"
He said, "Boo, you know I'm still trying to find the right work situation
it ain't my fault that THE MAN won't give me my propers, to be the head of a major corporation"
She said, "BABY you won't find a job looking in the classified and watching Ricki Lake
besides me and you, we got two mouths to feed and a lot more at stake"
He said "Boo, you know I've been trying, but the Man keeps holding me back
so that's why I look in the classified to find a good job, you don't understand my plan of attack"
She said, "Baby, it's ok to have a plan but you must put it into action
you can make excuses or money, not both, with you staying home I get no satisfaction"
He said "what you saying Boo, I ain't doing my part as head of this household?
you just don't understand me, you're always nagging me, if the real truth be told"
She said, "Baby, get your act together and stop blaming everything on the MAN

It's YOU who doubts himself, makes excuses, and gives
up every chance he can!"
He said, But Boo, Baby
"But Boo Baby Hell!," she said, I'm not listening to no
more lies or taking your mess any more
and if you won't be the man I know you are and *can be,*
pack your stuff and walk out the door,
"I'm tired of being patient, scrimping and saving, doing
without,
and this YOU MUST understand
you can't blame your failures and lack of initiative on
nobody else,
because YOU TOO ARE A MAN!"

Focus on the Positives

when the problems of the day
simply refuse to go away
when negative actions of so-called friends abound
and quality people of purpose can't be found
when crisis after crisis tend to tug at your heart
leading you to pose the question "am I really that smart?"
focus on the positives - forget about the negatives
when you wait for THAT call but the phone never rings
when you encounter friends of past loves and bad news
is all they bring
when your generosity and kindness is constantly abused
leaving you somewhat frustrated, dumbfounded, and
totally confused
focus on the positives - eliminate the negatives
always realize that you have a GOOD heart

you're a professional person, intelligent, charming and incredibly smart
you've overcome every obstacle that life has thrown your way
therefore you must NEVER get caught up in the negatives of what others do and say
focus on the positives - forget about the negatives

Back in the Day

I wonder what the young folks of today would have to say if they had to live their lives in every way
like we had to back in the day!
back in the day when Children had Respect for every adult
back in the day when children wouldn't talk back, they wouldn't insult
their parents, their neighbors, not even strangers they'd meet
children knew their PLACE and addressed every adult by Mister or Miss on their street
I wonder what the young folks of today would do
especially if they really and truly knew
that for being disrespectful to any adult, their parents could and would beat them black and blue
but now the laws tie a parents hands and punishing your child is of no use
because if you yell at or spank your child they can have you brought up on charges of child abuse
Yes, I wonder what the young folks of today would do

If they had to display good manners, and conduct and do exceptionally well in school
most of the young folks of today are spoiled, selfish, and the center of their own universe
back in the day we were expected to be the leaders of tomorrow and never expect the worst
we were expected to EARN, not DEMAND respect from everyone we would meet
not have an attitude, carry a gun, and be ready to shot anyone who bumped into us on the street
I haven't given up hope on today's youth and one-day the trouble makers among them will find
that there is a lot of truth in that old saying, "a hard head makes for a soft behind"

Black Robed Blues

Nine judges all dressed in black
making decisions that could set Black folks back
back to the days when Jim Crow was the rule
back to suffering and shuffling and being denied admittance to school
back to slaving from "can't see in the mornin' to can't see at night"
back to being the last hired, first fired and losing the vote which is our right
back, way back to separate but equal
back to KKK terrorism and making lynching's legal
and now the courts are ruling in favor of plaintiffs claiming reverse discrimination
one of our OWN? on the Supreme Court stopping righting the wrongs of our victimization

well this misguided BOY and his friends are determined to keep Black folk in the lower class
so should he continue to vote against his own kind, he can politely KISS MY A__!

I want to mend your Broken Heart!

He made a terrible mistake
When your heart he chose to break
From you his infidelity he foolishly thought he could hide
Telling you your suspicions of his other women he would not abide
Then one day you got proof, hmm............. Proof POSITIVE!
So you made up your mind, that with him you could no longer live
If only I knew you then I would have tried desperately to erase
each and every tear that he caused to stream down your lovely face
I would have been there to console you, caress you, telling you everything will be alright
reassuring you of your self worth, your goodness, and beauty with all my might
But I am just coming into your life, just now appearing on your radar screen
I can, and am willing to be that as close to perfect man, the one of whom you dream
I am capable of being both good to and for you and show you a love beyond compare
But first we must get to know one another better before a romance between us can go anywhere

I want to take you out many times so you can truly get to know me
What I know you'll discover is I am someone who'll Always be there for you, constantly
Someone who will be an asset as opposed to a liability
Someone who can and will provide you with true love, devotion and pure honesty
But only you can determine if my dreams of being with you ever come true
I hope and pray every day that I am not too late to both find and build a love supreme with you
Only you can give me a chance to prove that which I say...
Only time will tell
I will continue to Ask God that you'll take the time to get to know me, VERY WELL!

Some Sista's wouldn't know a good brother if they tripped over Him!

I want to make it clear, first and foremost this poem ain't about ME!
But it's about a GOOD brother who all his life was told he was ... well, UGLY
He'd be the first to admit that he's not a handsome guy
But he's well educated, a compassionate professional, who's generous to a fault, and excruciatingly shy
but the Sista's his whole life, ... overlooked his myriad good qualities
opting to pursue brothers whose only goal was to be Mr. Playa Playa,
guys who when it came to women were just plain greedy
the love them and leave them brothers were the first the Sista's would pursue
This UGLY but Decent brother was ignored, a brother they never knew, consequently any chance to be happy with him they obviously BLEW!
NO! He hasn't given up on the Sista's, and pursuing women of another race
He's just in a period of retrospection and retrenchment, in an emotional Hiding Place!
Waiting for that SPECIAL, Righteous Sista to appear on his radar screen
So he can envelope, saturate, and overwhelm her with a love SUPREME
You see even though the Sista's ain't paid this brother no attention
His ultimate and lifelong goal is to give a Sista a love devoid of rejection
A love that's totally immersed in devotion and perfection

The love he'd have for her would be more addictive than crack cocaine
cause her name would ALWAYS be on his lips, her mental image encoded in his brain
loving this Sista would be his lifelong Resolution
and to him for her there NEVER, EVER, could be a suitable Substitution
But this Brother's pragmatic,
he knows the Sista he's looking for is just a beautiful dream
Now he's All man, a Real Man, but his futile search makes him want to scream
He's 99.9% positive that his chances of finding the Sista of his dreams are very slim
Because he knows, like I know,
Some Sista's wouldn't know a good brother if they tripped over Him!

Relationships: The Good, the Bad, and the Ugly

The Good
Two people communicating on an intellectual plane
A physical love between them that's almost profane
Openly sharing even their most intimate insecurities
Returning their love to each other through the principal of reciprocity
Two people blessed by God with the ultimate expression of love
They're on the same spiritual track, their relationship ordained from above
Able to resolve their differences without causing each other any sorrow
Loving one another more today than yesterday, ... but not as much as tomorrow
A relationship that could survive in a mansion or a rundown shack in the hood
A relationship to be envied because it's loving, blessed, sincere, and Good

The Bad
Two people with only one or two things in common
Things get tough, ... their relationship they'll quickly abandon
A relationship that's based solely on "Good" sex and or money
Both looking for a relationship upgrade, saying "I shoulda been more patient, more choosey"
Neither looking for true love only trying to take as much as they can
Hindsight being 20/20 from the instant they met ... from their lover they should have ran

Away! ... as if they were soaked in gasoline and set on fire
The more time spent together the less respect one for the other, the less the desire
Avoiding each other's calls, making excuses, always irritated, it's just too sad
That people get involved in relationships from the outset they know will end up Bad

The Ugly
Two people who everyone they know questions "why are they together?"
Some powerful glue must've been used because each could do a lot better
They fuss, cuss, and fight everyday as if that's what relationship are all about
Their mental and physical health are certainly and increasingly in doubt
He can't STAND Her! and She can't STAND him!!!!
Everyday the prospect of their relationship surviving grows very slim
Staying with each other because of the kids, or the clothes, or the house or the car
Despising the sight of each other, their relief, cozying up with someone else at the bar
In relationships God promotes love instead strife, wanting us to be content and happy
NOT to be constantly at one another's throats, in a relationship that's vicious and very UGLY!

Relationship are never easy to maintain
So it's very important that before starting one we all refrain

From selecting our future love based on our own distorted selection process
We MUST first consult the Almighty to help us avoid another relationship mess

We need to humble ourselves before the Lord, and get down on our knees and pray
"Lord, please bless me with my special someone to love, honor and obey,"
So before hooking up with that "Special One" there is an immediate need
To ask God to anoint our relationships, ... because it's then and only then they will ever succeed!

He Just Keeps on Blessing Me!

When I'd spent my last money trying to impress my Saturday night date
that the next morning I couldn't tithe or put a Dime in the collection plate
even when my conduct throughout the week was so BAD his forgiveness I did not rate
He Just Keeps on Blessing Me!
When I was driving home from the "Club" knowing I was D-U-I
and the State Trooper pulled alongside me, glared at me, but passed me by
and I promised God I won't let this happen again as I let out a deep sign

He Just Keeps on Blessing Me!
When I've been reunited with people I haven't seen in 30 or more years
our reunion leads to our sharing our insights, dreams, and even our fears
and looking at where we are now from where we've been almost brings us to tears
He Just Keeps on Blessing Me!
When revenge envelopes my mind when an insult or betrayal I won't let pass
he reminds me my enemies' actions are due to envy and jealously
because they're in their own personal and moral morass
and I am reminded that he's ALWAYS helped me my enemies to Surpass
He Just Keeps on Blessing Me!
when I forget to thank him or Bible Study I conveniently forget to attend
when my Pastor's sermon I know is about me but I pretend not to comprehend
when I know that the people I am blessed to be related to and are friends with are indeed a Godsend
when I know he has every right my numerous blessings to suspend
and I know that as long as I am alive he's my very best friend
Because God Just keeps on Blessing Me!

Let Me Live My Life

Be a guiding light. to those who have lost their way
Be a crutch for those who need a little help standing on their own today
Give a helping hand to those who've fallen down
Give up, exchange a smile to those you meet who are wearing a frown
Lend your time instead of your money to someone in need
Lend your Christ like services to others, let this be your Christian creed
Forgive those who would mistreat, deceive, and lie on you
Forgive them because like the folks in the Bible, they know not what they do
Learn to pray as often when times are good as when things are going bad
Learn to put your trust in the Lord and it's guaranteed that your mood will go from sad to glad
Put your trust and faith in the Lord always relying on his love and mercy
Put your fears and concerns in the Lords hands asking daily "Lord please bless me!"
Look inward then toward the heavens avoiding negative folks, never become irate
Look forward to one day meeting your loved ones at the pearly gates
Live like you were Jesus not allowing fame, or fortune to lead you astray
Live a life full of kindness, and mercy, as if tomorrow was going to be your judgment day!

When I Think of YOU

When I think of you
I think of a loving, positive, God ordained relationship,
A relationship that is long over due.
When I think of you
I think of stimulating, Holy Spirit led conversations,
Conversations about the future, together
not our past that made us blue.
When I think of you
I think of the warmth of your embrace,
The tremendous pleasure derived from looking at your lovely face
That leads me to desire a relationship full of love, a love that is true
These are just a few of the things I think about...
When I think of you

True Love Ain't Conditional

She was totally and constantly confused
her worldview shaped by how bad she had been mistreated and abused
in her search for true love she lived a promiscuous past
got married then divorced, engaged - unengaged,
involved in too many one night stands that never seemed to last
then she met a spiritual, intelligent, kind, generous brother like me
someone who wanted to share everything with her and help her to be free:

free of all the negativity, physical and mental abuse
free of the deceptions, game playing and attempts to negate, diminish and reduce:
her self esteem, all her dreams to be truly happy for the rest of her life
her desire to be a good companion, best friend and a loving and devoted wife
but in her mind an extremely delinquent bill was due and someone had to pay
so she always kept me at arm's length and if I got too close she would stray, far away
when she introduced me to her co-workers, friends, and family
they all believed I was just a buddy, an acquaintance, no one she would be involved with seriously
but when we went on trips together people addressed us as husband and wife
we obviously appeared to them as a loving couple, one whose relationship was void of strife
I foolishly let her dictate where we ate, what movies we watched and the locales of all our vacations
but giving her this leeway all she did was to remind me of what in her mind were my limitations
She told me I could not have Thanksgiving dinner with her and her family at her sister's place
This was another of her attempts to play me, betray me, oh what a disgrace!
the lame and insane excuse was I did not eat pork so her sister would be offended
I felt like "she obviously thinks I am an idiot" It's time for this love affair to be ended
I foolishly relented, stayed with her and subsequently asked her to marry me

Her response was, "marriage is a big step, and my ex-husband well..."
It was then I realized that I had to be free
Free of her self centeredness, her lack of propriety, commitment and self esteem
Yeah, it was then that I realized that she was not the one God sent to me, not the woman of my dreams
They say time heals all wounds and for a long time I was mentally in the emotional ICU
But I have fully recovered, God has blessed me, lifted me higher, I am no longer feeling blue
I do thank God for the experience with her because I have learned to be patient, and to be still
Because when God is ready, when the time is right,
he will send me someone based upon his Divine will!

Your Cousins

Who comes to the backyard cookout with a six pack of beer minus four cans
Who pushes their way to the front of the food line being disrespectful to the elderly, and women,
Who stacks their plates so high you can't see their face and gets back in line time and time again
Who when they leave wraps up several plates to go with aluminum foil, and to get the accumulated food home requires a minivan
Your Cousins

Who has no home training and wears a hat inside at movies, concerts, or cabarets with a toothpick behind their ear

Who hasn't figured out how to put their cell phone on vibrate,
so when their cellphone rings they answer, talk throughout the indoor event and everything they say the people sitting near them can clearly hear
Who goes to an exclusive nightclub, wearing $250 sneakers, $500 blue jeans and all the other Hip Hop gear
Who gets angry when they are denied admittance when the printed dress code says,
"Proper attire required, no denim, no gym shoes no sportswear,
I repeat the dress code is crystal clear
Your Cousins

Who goes to the club in a dress so tight they look like 100 lbs. of potatoes in a 50 lb. sack
Who has a tattoo record of all their ex-boyfriends covering their breast that also goes half way down their back
Who's strutting their stuff at the club and orders a "Henny and Coke" "Corny-ak"
Who leaves their 5 kids by five different baby's daddy's home alone with nothing substantial to eat but some too sweet Kool Aid and assorted snacks
Your Cousins

Who comes to your house, helps you drink all your liquor and when you say, "let's get another bottle" never have any money to chip in
Who always asks you for a ride home, you do it for months,
but when you are low on cash and ask for a few dollars for gas only offer you a toothy grin

Who is always telling you how one day they're going to be rich
and take the whole neighborhood out on the town but their plan they've yet to begin
Who's always scheming, deceiving, and ripping off the people who are supposed to be their friends
Your Cousins

Who needs to get right with God and always do the right thing
Who should get better educated to use their God given talents
so to others joy and happiness they could bring
Who's on a fast track to Hell unless they give up on their frequent, repetitive sins like their weekend flings
Who needs to get down on their knees, pray and realize that Jesus is the King of Kings
Your Cousins

Haters

Haters got mad at me because I paid attention in school
now they're mentally bankrupt, underemployed,
uneducated alcohol and substances abusers,
you know that ain't even cool

Haters smile in my face but badmouth me behind my back
choking on their envy, and petty jealousies wishing they could BE where I'm at
no desire, motivation to do what I did to get what I got,
character, integrity, mental toughness, morals,
intelligence are the qualities I posses that they lack
I repeat they spend all day talking about me behind my back

Haters always saying, "he ain't this and he ain't that"
If they'd only spend as much time on improving themselves as they do talking about me
maybe they'd realize I'm not the only one whose being both talked about and laughed at

Haters act as if I'm taking every morsel of food off their plate
or as if I had stolen away from them their beloved soul-mate
Haters are vicious, insecure, evil folks who constantly lie in wait
for opportunities to lie on me, my character to desecrate and denigrate

You see Haters have haters that is just a universal rule

I don't hate on somebody else because of what they got
or because they were successful in school
I'm too busy increasing my knowledge, investments,
because I know money ain't nothing but a tool
Hating makes absolutely no sense to me because hating
don't buy me nothing and it ain't cool!
it's the silly, useless, retarded pastime of an ignorant fool

So if you are within the sound of my voice and are hating
on me
You need to get a life, do something positive, take a deep
breath... and count to three
Open a book called the Bible and let the Word of the Lord
help set you free
Of all your pettiness, envy, jealously and most importantly
your stupidity

It is not me who is your problem but the person you see
in the mirror every day
It is not me who is always saying I wish I hada, I shoulda ,
I woulda, I coulda much to your dismay
If you think I am too blessed maybe you need to do what I
do, ... Hey - I Pray!

Pray that God will bless you, keep his hedge of protection
around you and from His presence you will never stray
You see the secret to my success is that the words of the
Lord I earnestly try to obey
And as I go through this life it is Christian character,
demeanor, manner and lifestyle I display!
So if you are going to hate on me for what God has, is
and will do for me-Then HATE AWAY!

♪ Haters - How many of us have them?

Medgar Evers Died for Your Sins

a young brother standing in front of a party store was overheard to say
"don't be looking for me at no polling place on election day,
cause my **one vote** ain't gonna make a difference in **my neighborhood,**
crime, bad schools, poverty everywhere and there is no likelihood,
of me ever making it out, **so I'm keeping it real**
you folks who talk about voting **don't know the deal."**
But an older, wiser brother at the same spot was heard to say
"naw! young blood, ... its that attitude that causes you to stay
in neighborhoods where crime, poverty, and illiteracy abound
cause in hoods where people **vote,** rarely are those conditions found!"
"you see, people who **vote** select those folks who make all the decisions
haven't you seen whose on the Circuit and Supreme Court on television?
them folks was appointed by people who somebody **voted in**
and these judges are obligated to the ones who appointed them,
no matter how **slim** the election's victory margin
so you want to be one of them politicians, and judges are obligated to
cause if you look around, the following you'll see and find to be true:

people who are elected decide who does or does **NOT** go on welfare
whose kids **don't** get or get the best educations and breath clean air
whose sons and daughters are sent or not sent to wars in faraway lands
whose kids are expelled or whose kids just simply get a reprimand
who goes to a Country Club Prison or who's sent to the electric chair! ....
so young blood, **voting** is our way to try to make **everything** for **everybody fair!**"
"Tell me something young blood, you ever hear of the NRA?
Well they **VOTE** religiously to get their way, but why doesn't the NWA?
I'm old enough to know **Voting** ain't a **right** it's a **privilege**
our folks have sacrificed and died to get it ... so not **voting** is a **sacrilege!**
so if you refuse to register and vote young blood your people you'll be doing in
and people like Medgar Evers and countless others, **will have died for your sins!**

She likes the Brotha's

She likes the brotha's with the playa style of dress
But they lack good manners, sophistication, and finesse
She likes the brotha's with the thug, rough neck mentality, and it's a sin
Because they only wanted to use and abuse her, then never call her again
She likes the fast, smooth talking brotha's who in their big caddy take her for a spin
Their only interest was a 3-6 month bedroom liaison, now she's alone, dejected just another one of their "has beens"
She likes the brotha's who haven't read a book since High School because they're "keeping it real"
They can't mentally give her what they ain't got. because reading, writing, and intellectual stimulation for them lacks appeal
She likes the brotha's who lavish her with money,
expensive gifts and travel to faraway places
In the final analysis they got more from her than they gave,
now she's left hugging her pillow at night longing for their embraces
She likes the brotha's who from the outset had no good intention
Now she's popping pills at night to sleep and others to relieve her of her tension
She likes the brotha's who would never put a $15k ring on her finger while down on one knee
I guess that's why she'd never ever fall in love with a spiritual
intelligent,

well educated,
sophisticated,
charming
generous,
devoted,
and truly loyal brotha like Mel

My X's: A Poem Dedicated to the Composite of Some of the Women I Have Dated

What the Hell could've I been thinking
can't blame it on the fact that when we first met I was drinking
Remy VSOP, straight up water back
but after dealing with your craziness for 6 plus years I just had to give up on the Cognac
and I'd probably be better off if I was doing Crack
because at least the Crack would temporarily ease my mental pain
that stems from an unrewarding, useless, pitiful love for you that nearly drove me insane
a love for you that you absolutely, positively refused to reciprocate
a debilitating, degrading love for you I could not shake until it was much too late
a love where you probably had 2 - 3, nah! maybe 6 other lovers on the side
and all the while I foolishly longed for the day you'd be my bride
but after investing myself totally into loving you it became crystal clear to me
that you only wanted to use - abuse - - confuse this brother because you lacked any semblance of what love truly is and any sense of propriety
but I finally came to my senses and made a hasty retreat forcing you to find yet another victim to play on because in the final analysis you don't even know how to be discreet
so I just wanted you to know per your request I've moved on permanently

found me a regular church going, beautiful, sensual,
loving, well educated, 6 figure income, good job having
sister, and Oh, by the way,
she also exudes and demonstrates a major degree of
spirituality
so please don't think my comments are petty, vindictive,
even hating on you or a parting shot
because if the truth be told, I'm just here to tell you she's
none of the things you are
and **EVERYTHING YOU'RE NOTIIII**

Should I?

Just got word that another good friend has just died
saw one another in the mall last week - he told me about his numerous strokes,
so happy to see one another we both almost cried
With so many young people my age dying and leaving here
Should I be concerned if I'm next? - should I be consumed with fear?
Should I live the rest of my life as if each day might be my last?
Should I try to atone for all the bad things I'd done in my past?
Should I try to make up for lost time, payoff all my bills get caught up on my rent?
Should I take a retrospective look over my life - was it a life well spent?
Should I go home, go to bed laying in a fetal position and just wait for judgment day
Should I realize just how good God has been to me - should I get down on my knees and pray?
Should I come to the realization that even if tomorrow is my last day here on earth that God has given me the ultimate gifts, His Son, the Holy Spirit, my family
and friends all of which I've had since the day of my birth
Should I be like the Epicureans, "eat, drink and be merry," leaving my family in a financial lurch
or Should I start thinking about my morals, salvation, eternal life and start going to church
Should I realize how good God has been to me - start being sincere and nice to everyone I meet

Should I stop being ego-centric and start helping others like the brother sleeping in the street
Should I finally get my act together, live a Christian life before it's too late
Cause I'm sure when my time comes I want to be on the inside of the Pearly Gates!

About the Author

"Brother James" aka: Henry James was born and reared in Louisville, Kentucky. He is the second eldest of eight children of the late Reverend Robert W. James and Juanita Mae Alexander James. He was educated in the Louisville Public School System.

He is an avid reader of history (African and African American, and World history), Religion, Political Science, Philosophy, Behavioral Science and Psychology. He also enjoys various genres of music and has a massive book and music collection.

Front cover: A family celebration in 1947 at my father's sister's house in Louisville, Kentucky.

Pictured from left to right; My father's sister Leona, my father's father William James (aka Daddy Willie), my father, Robert Walter James, my oldest brother Robert Sylvester James sitting in my mother's lap, my Mother, Juanita Mae Alexander James, an unidentified family friend and my Mothers Mother, Carrie Porter (aka *Mother Porter*).

www.ingramcontent.com/pod-product-compliance
Lightning Source LLC
Chambersburg PA
CBHW061503040426
42450CB00008B/1471